UGLY GIRL POEMS BY HOLLY DAY

UGLY GIRL by Holly Day is published and printed in the USA by Shoe Music Press, Alpharetta, GA. ©2015 Shoe Music Press and Holly Day. All Rights Reserved.

Cover Image by Bill Hicks. ©2015 Bill Hicks

ISBN-13: 978-0692470206
ISBN-10: 0692470204

CONTENTS

All the Days After 1

I Tell Her 2

Inhale 3

Soft Tissue 4

Bleeding the Brakes Dry 5

The Meat Man's Wife 6

Unwinding 7

The Arrogant Imposter 8

Grandma and Grandpa at Home 9

The Night 10

Grieving for a Lost Child 11

Boots XV 12

Reverberations 13

Tall Drunk Guy at the Bar 14

Trying to Go Home 15

This Isn't Love 16

After the Honeymoon 17

Sunshine 18

Love is Very Patient and Kind 20

Love Stinks 21

Candles 22

Arcade Priest 23

The Haunted 24

The Photographer's Notes 25

The Letters Keep Coming	26
Haunting	27
What Keeps You Going	29
All the Glitter	30
If You Want To Be Misguided	31
The Weight of Dirt	32
Freedom	33
What If	34
The Dance	35
Missing Keystrokes	36
Intervention	37
Disappointed	38
The First Time	39
Midnight Caller	40
Nocturnal Song	41
The Last Note	42
The Other Woman	43
The First Step	44
Thumbelina	45
What I Remember	46
Divine Beings and Their Creations	47

ACKNOWLEDGEMENTS

* "The Meat Man's Wife" appeared in *Sweet Ass #11* and *Spooge Extroosions #1*
* "Grandma and Grandpa at Home" appeared in *Dreams and Nightmares #33*
* "Boots XV" appeared in *Philadelphia Poets Vol. 12 #1*
* "Reverberations" appeared in *Report To Hell #9* and *Quilt Vol. 18*
* "Tall Drunk Guy at the Bar" appeared in *Sugar Baby Rising #24*
* "Trying to Go Home" appeared in *Perimeter Vol. I #3* and *Laughing Boy Review #3*
* "This Isn't Love" appeared in *The Plastic Tower #24*
* "After the Honeymoon" appeared in *Real Change Vol. 5 #10*
* "Sunshine" appeared in *Real Change Vol. 5 #10* and *Blue Collar Review Vol. 3 #4*
* "Love is Very Patient and Kind" appeared in *Home Planet News #62*
* "Love Stinks" appeared in *Radio Void #11*
* "Candles" appeared in *Teen Anthem #1*

All the Days After

Days pass into weeks
and now even the flowers
are dead, curled brown in their vase like squirrel paws,
little hands. I call
my husband,
tell him to take

the vase full of withered
baby hands away. He
looks at me as if
he has something

he wants to say to me but
doesn't dare. Instead, he
takes the vase off the nightstand, takes
it out of
the house. I

can hear the trash can
lid outside slamming, metal
lid, metal can. I listen for his footsteps
downstairs, heavy boots
on wood, but
I fall asleep

sometime during the waiting.

I Tell Her

being a wife and being a mother are two very similar things,
as she watches me clean up crumbs after my husband.
I put my hands over her ears, fill her head instead with princes
that never stop blooming.

Every night, I could maybe see him as some sort of hero
contributing something to the family, the horrible things he calls me,
waking up the middle of the night with babies.
I don't believe this, but I still do it.

Inhale

My daughter lies in her crib screaming
some formless, aimless rage and I

suck angrily at my cigarette saying
I'm glad that I'm going to die someday,

picture her crying, silently reminiscing
over me lying back in a coffin, eyes closed.

I wonder if it's me she hates so much. I
don't understand a word she's saying.

Soft Tissue

The mummy comes to my door, tells me
he's moved in down the street, only now realized
we were neighbors, we should go out for coffee
sometime, we should catch up. Startled, not expecting
this shambling wreck of my past to just show up
on my doorstep as though nothing had ever
happened between us, I just nod my head,
say that would be nice.

I shut the door and my daughter asks
who I was talking to, asks why
I look so funny, so strange. I say nothing,
can't find the words to explain that sometimes
the dead can crawl their way out through layers of dirt,
breathe life back into their rotting limbs and
stop by for a visit, without any sort of warning,
no polite warning at all. I struggle

for an explanation, finally tell her
that it's really none of her business, that even mommies
have things in their past
that nice little girls shouldn't know about.

Bleeding the Brakes Dry

I can almost feel the warm water pooling
around my sore ankles, the burnt skin on the tops of my feet.
Far away is a safe place where tiny crustaceans wriggle beneath
my heel in time with the ebb of the tide. If I try hard enough

the rumble of waves crashing on a white sand beach are loud enough
that I can't hear the angry muttering in the garage, the sound
of my car being worked on by a husband that promised
to take me away from here, take me back to the ocean,
so long ago it might as well be a lie.

The Meat Man's Wife

It's an old game
that still gets me off—I lie
perfectly still
while he labels the pieces of my body
with a blue butcher's marker,
breaking me up into my fuckable parts.

He once told me
he used to work at a meat packing plant
and the only way he could stand touching the cold
cattle flesh
was to concentrate on images of naked women. Now,
he can only get turned on if he pretends
his women are dead animals.
Or so he says.

The cold marker cuts my breasts
into twin racks of ribs, my back
into prime cuts, shoulder roasts. The steel cuffs
feel like barbed hooks poised
to pierce my flesh—I await
the tug of the crane arm lifting me up—suspending
me,
helpless, in the dark.

Unwinding

I know time has passed
because my reflection has been replaced
by the face of a stranger. The daffodils and tulips
have disappeared under flurries of overnight snow, and I have finished
all of my imaginary conversations, imaginary letters.
We had a lot to talk about.

There is no small talk, I don't know
where to start. I tell you I miss the pitter patter of tiny feet
because I know that even our children are older.
I refuse to acknowledge the wild-haired, gray-eyed woman
across from me because
it couldn't have been that long ago.

The Arrogant Imposter

He ate, pushing his fork into the pile of spaghetti
in front of him with a fervor that seemed
too angry for dinner. He was nervous, my father
was out of town and he
was not supposed to be there.

My mother watched him eat with the look of
a contented lioness in her eyes, this was her
plan come true, her lover at the table with us,
her children, we could pretend to be a family
while my dad was gone. He tried to engage me

in talk about school, about what I wanted to be
when I grew up, what sorts of things I liked,
smiling too big as my mother's knee touched his
under the table. I could only think about all the things I wanted to say,
all the wrong answers that would have worked
just right for his questions.

Instead my mind went blank, my tongue numb, when I
saw him take my mother's hand.

Grandma and Grandpa at Home

The old man on top of the hill watches
porno films every day while his wife
is busy shopping, spending his hard-earned
retirement money on new drapes for the
bathroom.

He fantasizes daily about his
old woman bursting into the TV
room wearing nothing but leather
underwear and a pair of thigh-high
stiletto
boots she bought at the sleazy
sex shop downtown.

Sometimes he sees her in a bright red
rubber bikini, the G-string going
up the crack of her ass and
sometimes she's wearing a pink lace teddy or
a white silk camisole.

Every day he thinks of her dressed
like this and every day she comes home
with packages full of drapes
or scented soaps or presents for the
kids he can't remember or sometimes a new
housecoat.

The Night

We didn't want to see the body,
the smell was coming from her apartment
and our mother had shot herself.

I said I wanted proof she was dead.
I asked, "Are you sure you burned the right body?"
The urn was so small. Copper, tastefully etched.

Later, my brother and I got so drunk
we got into a fight, took it out to the street.
I tried to hit him and missed.

Grieving for a Lost Child

He tells me he still wonders.
He sometimes still thinks about the baby we lost.

I can tell he thinks of it often. I remind him
it's pointless to dwell on, that tiny mass of gray flesh.

He thinks I'm a cold, callous bitch, tells me so,
and we start drinking in earnest, in silence.

I want to comfort him with trite clichés about the circle of life,
that one in every five pregnancies is doomed,

that we already have two wonderful children.
I know what to say, but I know he doesn't want to hear it.

Boots XV

Someday, reporters will ask you what you did during the war. The
Child's arms were around the waist of his mother's dress.
This will all fade to yearly get-togethers with old army buddies. She

Won't recognize you as an adult. Bombs set just over the next hill, she wore
A blue dress. You remember. The bombs went off in the wrong direction. When
The sun came up, everyone was dead. All the old ghosts will be replaced by
new ones. She

Will fade away with the rest of the memories. She
Will fade away with the rest of the memories. Someday, when
You are older, a woman will trace the long white scars you wear

On your back and ask you where they came from. She
Will ask you what you did during the war. Her dress
Will be the same color blue as the one worn by the woman on the hill. The

Long white scars on your back will not fade away. The
White of the little boy's eyes were hidden by the woman's dress.
His skin peeled away like the flesh of a potato. She

Never did fall down, not while you were looking. She wore
A dress the color the sky was once, the way it looked when
You were just a boy yourself.

If your children are born with no arms and legs, will it seem unfair?
If your own children die, as children, will it seem unfair?

Reverberations

Though children may outgrow, forget
cruelty of youth, I will not forget
the Ugly Girl, the ugly, horrible names
I've had, christened not by Mom and Dad but faces
whose names slip my mind but
stick in my mind.

Make me hard, make me cold, make me
dead to taunts from long ago—it was me
against the entire class, the entire
city, the entire
world.

Though children bloom into cautious adults
and find new ways to express their hate, as adults
I find it hard to believe
they've banished the Ugly Girl from their dreams,
the names that jabber in my sleep.

Make me invisible, make me pretty.
Sadistic God, like You made other girls normal and pretty
and sane—oh, sweet Sanity! To be happy
with myself is such an idealistic dream. I want
to be happy with myself for just
one
whole
dream.

Tall Drunk Guy at the Bar

He said "I don't like short girls,
how they crawl all over your body like a
sot little ant, I can't deal with the way
my own body feels
with little girls."

He shudders, and I feel
an incomprehensible desire
to crawl up the length of his leg,
across the expanse of his belly and chest
and sit on his shoulder, wrap my arms
around his face and
lick the sweat off his forehead.

Trying to Go Home

Everything my mother had told me, prepared me
for, the feeling of Home that should overwhelm,
overpower, this land
of my warrior ancestors should set me at peace
with my self, for once,

but I can't sleep here. The nights
are too quiet, the people
are all inbred, like a chunk of Midwest America
set free to drift in the Atlantic.
I already knew what superstitious farm-folk were like

four thousand miles ago. I wrote my mother
to tell her
of her mistake
but my neighbor claims the government censors
all negative mail.

This Isn't Love

We will not get through this.
There are only so many people
I can be for you
and I have to be myself now.

We will not get through this.
I will never be the person
you want to wake up to, I will never be
in your dreams.

And I am dying here. I am falling
apart
at the mannequin joints. I
have made a mess of everything
good, was there ever anything or am I…?

We will not get through this.
We have nothing left to build upon,
nothing left to work with, try for.
We have nothing left to talk about.
We will not get through this.

After the Honeymoon

Razor-sharp spider webs crisscross rays of
white moonlight, broken glass windowpanes
and stained glass skin—mommy listen,
listen when I tell you
he has a temper, he has quite
a temper.

Razor-sharp porcelain fragments on
bloodstained linoleum, purple skin fading
to dark red, under ice—oh mommy listen,
listen to me when I tell you
I have to get out of here, I have to
get out.

Sunshine

This sandwich is good.
I made it myself. Ham and cheese. Wheat
and rye.
I'm going to eat it now.
I have to leave this place.

Too many walls in a building. Too many exit
signs leading to locked doors.
Too many windows that cannot be opened.
Too many voices screaming in my
head on the phone on the intercom, it's all just
a bunch of words and I
refuse to understand them anymore.

It's such a nice day.
I think I'll eat my sandwich outside. There,
beneath the tree.
A black dog shares my shade.
I'm going to die here.

It's the simplicity of memos. It's the arrogance
of middle management.
It's the concept of "superiors." It's a denial
of my peers.
It's the way my high heels catch
on the loose stacks of carpet,
the way my pantyhose stretches to snag
and snap like
snaky ripped tendons
up the backs of my legs.

It's the charred bullet hole I had to put
in my head
to get all this corporate verbiage out.

Go away, black dog.
I will not share my sandwich with you.

Love is Very Patient and Kind

It's true
I slept through the whole
procedure, remember nothing
solid
but the faint whirring of a vacuum pump
slowing to a sputtering stop, or the beginning
few seconds of the IV drip
blurring the lines between the ceiling tiles.

But I can feel the holes being hollowed out
inside me, late at night, trying to sleep,
hear the click of metal on flesh
fingers on my thighs, see
what it must have been like for the doctor

to hold all my hopes and dreams in one
white-gloved hand, so small
it would have barely
covered her palm.

Love Stinks

As
she sat
there in a
self-destructive
hypnotic stupor reflecting
on her lower-than-usual feelings
of self-worth she noticed a disembodied
hand crawling towards her from across the
bathroom floor. The hand slid in between her legs
and up her skirt finding a home at least inside her, deep
inside of her. "Is this what it's like to be crazy?" she asked
herself, tense, scared, but also curious and lonely, quickly relaxing
as the hand began to move in an ever-so-familiar pattern, a pattern she
had never expected to feel again. "Why didn't you come back sooner?" she
moaned, remembering the good old days, before Charlie was more than just an
unclaimed unnamed file in the morgue, recognizable only by his custom-made
ultra-cool sunglasses and his class ring. The hand, of course, emitted no
intelligible reply, although if she could have understood sign
language they might have talked. But as it was, it was over
all too soon; she climaxed and the hand withdrew to
scuttle back to its unseen hole in the wall, minus a
fingertip. A month later, as she breathed in her
last, her lower torso a mass of purple and
black the sweet scent of gangrene ripe in
the air, the surgeon finally found the
incriminating fingertip, dirty nail
and all, swollen to gargantuan
proportions like a tampon
under a tap faucet, a yet-
unnamed shade of green.
There's gotta be a
moral around
here some-
where.

Candles

Talk like I'm clay beneath your words.
Talk like a surrogate father,
mold me into your dream image of woman.
Make me something I am not.

I melt beneath your logic, lose weight
to fit your fantasies,
cut my hair and talk respectfully,
eyes on the ground
when you talk back.

Just waiting for this chapter to end
so I can go on to another story,
incognito from one to the next.
Men are so predictable.

Arcade Priest

I've run out of quarters, out of my mind,
minutes from salvation, slowing to a stop—I'm going to let him do
it, do all those horrible things he says dumb
little girls have to do to get more quarters. I've been loved and rubbed

bare by all sorts of angels, buffed smooth from all angles,
scraped clean of my maliciousness and left empty inside.
I've been saved by the Devil from the side of the Lamb
and it is just not nearly enough for me to be
this close to salvation.

The Haunted

I can't seem to get rid of your voice
constant in my ear, the subtle constant
clicking and clacking of your
spoken vices and dreams, conversations that should

have ended when you walked out the
door but they never end, they
go on and on. See your face behind my closed
eyes as if you were tattooed on the insides of my

eyelids and not some haunting reconstruction
of memory, you cannot
be as beautiful as you are in
my dreams, I hope I pray that

as you walk through your day, smiling
pleasantly at strangers, that somewhere
pressed against your soul is
some painful, unshakeable photograph of me.

The Photographer's Notes

So profound, your disfigurement, I
can't help but wonder if
you were pretty once, whole, perhaps
in that long before when you were
prepubescent, a child, before you

grew into the angry adult

with all the bumps and scars
on the inside. Did once friendly hands,
friendly eyes, friendly voices look into
your innocent eyes and see
the happy, beautiful baby you were,
struggling to stifle the screams, the lost dreams, labored breath,
labored breath clinging to damp, dying lungs, struggling
to spit out those

last angry words at my
retreating back? I think about that lost child, I want
to be buried deep inside you, still, somewhere
in that dark fog I married, I
want him to be there.

The Letters Keep Coming

Cringe. Draw away from me out
of me, slough away
promises, burn holes
in dreams. I know
you, silent in the darkened hall, white armor
stripped and revealed to be paste. Tell me why
I need you. Don't leave me yet. Run. Pull

yourself off of me out of me get
as far as you can from
me, I exile you because
I know. Once a week

she calls me to let me know you're still
sleeping with her, tells me about
the life you have planned
for the two of you. She wants forgiveness.
She wants to know if I'm okay with all
of this.

I tell her I'm fine.

Haunting

I close my eyes and pretend
that you're not in my
head, that when I close my
eyes I don't still see you. I close
my ears and pretend that
I don't recognize your
voice, that I don't remember
how
your breath

sounds when you sleep, that I don't remember
you. Somehow you
got inside me and
I can't shake you
loose. Somehow I have to find
some way to purify

myself of all the things
you put inside of
me. Our last conversation
still floats through my dreams,
the cold creep of certainty
I felt when I knew it would be

our last, our last moments
as a couple. I could
see you pulling away
from me, even then, as
if in a dream, a
horrible dream, long

before you told me
you were leaving,

felt it as certain
as a door closing
between us.

What Keeps You Going

Close your eyes and concentrate,
and swing. Connect. Feel the way the blade slides so
clean through whatever
you touch, wherever you touch,
clean through. This is what warriors
do. This is who you are. Inhale
and hold your breath, exhale with the
kill. Feel your breath leave your body like the steam
of a train, of a steam engine, pushing

you forward to the end. All around you
is the end of the world, just beyond the darkness

of your eyelids. If you open your eyes you will be face-
to-face with
devastation, an empty room, so much blood. Keep
them closed forever, against the light, the tally of your
crimes, your task,
the things that will haunt you past death. Only soldiers
that keep their eyes closed will make it
past today, only you will make it past tomorrow.

Keep your eyes closed. Follow
the orders in your head.
Don't think about what just happened, what you
did, what you're going to do. Get a good night's
sleep. Keep your chin up.

All the Glitter

I must not have wanted to be beautiful, even with
the obvious primping and painstaking
attention to detail. I look at the photos of myself
from back then, try to remember who I was dressing for
and I can't. The woman in the photos
does not look like me, looks tired, angry,
guarded, eyes hidden by layers of black makeup,
face smoothed over by pancake makeup, blusher,
kabuki influences from late-night TV. I must not have loved
the person I was preening for, I think, or the people
I was going out to meet some place all those years ago, people
I can no longer remember.

If You Want To Be Misguided

Years ago she, beautiful, thought she was in
love but this is today and she hides in her house
afraid to answer the door, afraid of what the

neighbors would say if they saw. What would her mother say if she saw her
now? Would she recognize her child? Would she see her daughter?
She shuffles past the covered windows peering through. The drapes that
hide her from the sun. She is all alone in

here and she can take all the time she needs to walk from
one end of the house to the other end of the house.
Is that his key at the door? She runs

back to her bedroom and pretends she has been there
all day, a good wife just like he asked for.
She wouldn't dream of running away, leaving—she

stands in the darkness of the room and holds her breath, listens
for his footsteps. No one is there. She is alone.

The Weight of Dirt

Under the carved stones dotting
the soft hills, spaced every three feet, lies a woman
planting, dirt stuck to her dress legs, arms outstretched,
crossed, resisting still the

inexorable crush of
decay, eyes sewn shut, her hair perfectly coiffed,
tied in a small knot behind
her head, eyes still shut, unmoving, as the shovel tip
splinters wood.

He trusted her so completely, but then
she died, he says, leaning against the
handle, putting all of his weight behind the blade,
uncovering enough of the coffin to open
the lid, flashlight patient over her clothes as he
remembers the color of her eyes,
pulls the ring off of her finger,

to give to the next wife.

Freedom

When she got tired of dancing, she made her feet
still, made her arms
still, pulled. The strings
brought a rain
of bloody fingertips and thumbs.
They fell in a pile around her. She thought
how could these sad, pale, still-wriggling snakes
ever have been in control?

The marionette sat on a hill of clean-cut
phalanges, arms around her knees, contemplating
her first sunrise as a free thing. She
could go anywhere now, she knew. She could
walk away from this, she could find a new hand
to move her arms and legs, a hand
belonging to someone who might on occasion ask her
"Where would you like to go now?" She

could even tie her strings to a bird,
some great, ocean-traversing albatross
and fly away.

What If

If one of us was to move away, what would
happen to the other piece
of the puzzle that makes up our neighborhood, would
the people who move into your empty house

fit in as well with my own hopes and dreams? When that
day comes, when the moving trucks pull up to take
away every trace of you and your family, will I
be able to stand the empty look

of the windows of your house
that first night?

The Dance

You've finally caught her, across the room, promises of
fairy tale castles and big screen love-
scenes in your eyes—I remember being her, once
in the days before I became a rotting corpse
waiting by the telephone, in the dark, in
our bed, always waiting for you
to come back home.

One last pastel-colored cocktail and she is yours for-ever, or just tonight,
whatever you decide her role
will be. She glides through the walls of
human flesh toward you as if summoned, and here, far
away, I know exactly what you are
thinking, lying here, rotting from my hollow places
begging for just one last bite from
your hard, sharp axe, before you
plow me under.

Missing Keystrokes

A typewriter lies dead in the corner
on the floor, keyboard split, askew, like a mouthful
of angry teeth inlaid with
carefully-set pieces of ebony screaming
"Hit me again you
qwerty motherfucker."

A typewriter burns bright in the corner, tapering
flames darken the single sheet of paper still
stuck in the dented rubber roller, one
word burning brighter than the rest taunts
"happily" asks "are you happy now?"

Intervention

I dream
of running away and joining
a cult, or a church, some place where
I can lose myself completely in
fake religion, pure religion, the dreams
of one crazy person with enough hope and love for us, all
of humanity. These are the days

I fantasize about stigmata, marking myself
with real bloody holes caused by fake god
intervention, fantasize
about speaking in tongues, kissing snakes,
being found on the stoop of kind
missionaries, these are the days

I dream of not being me.

Disappointed

He went crazy while I was still
at work. His friends had come over for lunch, saw him
go from reasonably odd to completely insane in
a matter of minutes. Our son was sleeping in his crib,
otherwise they would have left, too.
I came in the door after
a long day at work, saw him pacing, pacing,
lecturing wildly and waving his arms around his
head like he was trying to scare off
invisible flies.
"He's all yours now," his friends said when
they saw me, shaking their heads in sympathy but
not wanting
to get involved. Ten

years later, I'm sitting in court, telling
stories of how things went from bad to worse.
"I don't remember any of this," says the husband.
"I haven't seen our son since he was two years old.
I'd like to apologize for
anything I did to you back then." The lawyers smile at me
as if this will make it all better, will excuse the violent fights,
the things he stole from me, the nights I slept with my son
curled up in my arms, afraid
of what was coming next.

The First Time

He said I was making
him crazy, he said I
was too
young to be spending so much time
at his house, ditching school to
watch TV

with him, still wearing the old
sweat pants he slept
in the night before.
He said

I was too pretty
to waste my time hanging out with
an old man, that I should
try to meet a boy my
own age. But I knew
those boys would
never talk to me.

Midnight Caller

At night the
angry thud of the
dishwasher

sounds like monsters.
The groan
of the house quietly settling sounds like

prowlers.
I can almost see the deranged face
of my family's murderer pressed against

the glass
sliding doors.

Nocturnal Song

If I could have accepted that this morning
we would be ended and done not later
than tonight I never would have gotten up,
exposed myself to the morning.
I would have stayed asleep, alive

under the covers, reserved my arm, numb
around your upper body, lips on your back,
eyes stopped up. I would have found a way to contain

the dawn, to keep the bright fingers of light
from creeping across the bedclothes to trace the shadows
of your face, to stroke your eyelids into opening, to keep
this new thought that we must be over from
blossoming into the angry flower

you keep close to your heart,
this denial of me.

The Last Note

If Houdini could not make it back
from the afterlife
to let his waiting wife know he had crossed over
that there was a heaven
or that he was in hell
or nothing at all
then you should not expect to hear from me
after I'm gone. Leave no

spirit bells by the window for me to ring,
do not look for my face in the shadowed corners
reflected in mirrors, bring no
spirit-channelers to ghost-write one last
love letter to you from beyond the grave.

Don't look for me
for I won't be there.

The Other Woman

(Dim the lights a little more, gather your belongings,
leave. Fling a crimson rag on top of the bare bulb
next to the divan—wheel in the post-holocaust gag city mock-up
and permit the vermin to commence loping through the maze.)
I'm walking in your ideas, in a colorless seaside scene, naked feet
leaving no footprints in the sand. This chunk of ass

is the single solitary genuine human being here tonight. Wings
of seraph hammer against the glass windows of the inn, insensitive
to everything excluding our blind sins (pour a couple additional
pails of murder on the coastline, wrap up the distended cadavers,
destroy the rats.) I nearly telephoned you yet again last night,
imagining that the phone was right by your head, but I knew

that disgusting thing would be staying over for the weekend
and would pick up the phone, stockpiling your calls—I
enfolded the pink, synthetic die-cast receiver between my sodden thighs
and imagined I was hoarding sections of you through these hallucinations.
(The Armageddon recreation will go back to the beginning by itself
tomorrow. Let's call it a day. The conclusion of any epoch signifies

something has to die.)

The First Step

I take the piece of paper, put it
in my mouth, feel the word "love" dissolve in my saliva, in my blood,
and now I understand marriage.

The individual letters drift like little stones
throughout my body, break up like tiny meteors, turn to sand,
sink to my feet and

keep me here.

Thumbelina

There once was a woman who
prayed for just one little baby,
someone to love and call her own.
She didn't care if it was
a little boy, a little

girl. But the only baby
that answered her prayers was too
small, too quiet, curled tiny
in her palm. It would not move,
it did not cry. Morning came,

the woman
sat by the windowsill, rocking
a walnut shell cradle with
the tip of her finger, sang
songs of the places
her child would never see.

What I Remember

His letters unfold and flutter like
some codex written by a foreign hand, I don't
recognize his handwriting after all these years, can't
remember the things he said in the letters that made me
forgive and suppress so many things.

I can still picture him glaring at me
from across the room, face frozen in a stone frown
like some feathered Olmec death god, some devotee
from a severe mystery cult determined
to convert me to his way of thinking.

Divine Beings and Their Creations

I held my baby in my arms
for the first time and wondered,
am I mud or wood? Will I
crack or fade? Bend
or break? Or will I simply disintegrate

so gradually that only those who have known me
over brief snippets of elongated time
know if there is something different,
something wrong? Wrong? I felt
his tiny hands press into my skin
for the first time, felt those tiny, red fingers,
kitten-sharp nails, and I thought,

mud, definitely, this
is the thing that will finally
shape me into some semblance
of glory, fire me hard
into something stronger than beauty.

ABOUT THE AUTHOR

Holly Day has been writing professionally for over 26 years, and has had her poetry, short stories, and articles appear in over 3,000 professional high-circulation periodicals, e-zines, university literary magazines, fanzines, small press magazines, local weeklies, and audio-zines. She has been nominated for many Pushcart awards, several Dzanc Books Best of the Web awards, an Isaac Asimov Award, a 49th Parallel Award, and is the 2011 winner of the Sam Ragan Award for Poetry and a 2013 Plainsongs Award winner. She's also co-authored three fairly-successful Dummies guides (Music Theory for Dummies, recently translated into Dutch, French, Portuguese, Spanish, German, Polish, Persian, and Russian; Music Composition for Dummies, recently translated into German; and Guitar All-in-One for Dummies and Piano All-in-One For Dummies) and a few Minnesota-specific travel guides (Walking Twin Cities, Insider's Guide to the Twin Cities, and A Brief History of Nordeast Minneapolis). She also has several poetry books out by independent presses—most recently, *Late-Night Reading for Hard-Working Construction Men* (The Moon Publishing) and *The Smell of Snow* (ELJ Press). When she's not writing, she can be found at The Loft Literary Center in Minneapolis, Minnesota, where she's been a writing instructor for the past 14 years.